Ponies and Horses

Horses

Ponis y caballos

DK | Penguin Random House

FIRST EDITION
Series Editor Deborah Lock; **US Editor** John Searcy;
Project Art Editor Mary Sandberg; **Production Editor** Siu Yin Chan; **Production** Claire Pearson;
Jacket Designer Mary Sandberg; **Reading Consultant** Linda Gambrell, PhD

THIS EDITION
Editorial Management by Oriel Square
Produced for DK by WonderLab Group LLC
Jennifer Emmett, Erica Green, Kate Hale, *Founders*

Editors Grace Hill Smith, Libby Romero, Michaela Weglinski;
Spanish Translation Isabel C. Mendoza;
Photography Editors Kelley Miller, Annette Kiesow, Nicole DiMella;
Managing Editor Rachel Houghton; **Designers** Project Design Company;
Researcher Michelle Harris; **Copy Editor** Lori Merritt; **Indexer** Connie Binder;
Proofreaders Carmen Orozco, Larry Shea; **Reading Specialist** Dr. Jennifer Albro;
Curriculum Specialist Elaine Larson

Published in the United States by DK Publishing
1745 Broadway, 20th Floor, New York, NY 10019
Copyright © 2023 Dorling Kindersley Limited
DK, a Division of Penguin Random House LLC
22 23 24 25 26 10 9 8 7 6 5 4 3 2 1
001-336109-Aug/2023

A catalog record for this book
is available from the Library of Congress.
HC ISBN: 978-0-7440-8379-8
PB ISBN: 978-0-7440-8378-1

DK books are available at special discounts when purchased in bulk for sales promotions, premiums,
fundraising, or educational use. For details, contact: DK Publishing Special Markets,
1745 Broadway, 20th Floor, New York, NY 10019
SpecialSales@dk.com

Printed and bound in China

The publisher would like to thank the following for their kind permission to reproduce their images:
a=above; c=center; b=below; l=left; r=right; t=top; b/g=background

Alamy: Peter Llewellyn 17; **Corbis:** Walter Bieri / EPA 22; **Dreamstime.com:** Warangkana Charuyodhin 4-5,
Elena Titarenco 12, 13; **DK Images:** Miss. H Houlden ac, Stephen Oliver 2t, 8c; **FLPA:** Gerard Lacz 18–19; **Getty Images:**
Gallo Images / Travel Ink 6-7b; **Getty Images / iStock:** NiKita Filippov 20-21; **Masterfile:** R. Ian Lloyd 26-27; **Shutterstock:**
Picture Partners 9, Kondrashov MIkhail Evgenevich 16, Dennis Donohue 24-25; **SuperStock:** Age Fotostock 28-29

Cover images: *Front:* **123RF.com:** Olga Itina b; **Shutterstock:** Macrovector tr, br, Vector_Up;
Back: **Shutterstock:** Macrovector tl, cra, bl

All other images © Dorling Kindersley Limited
For more information see: www.dkimages.com

For the curious
www.dk.com

Ponies and Horses

Ponis y caballos

Fiona Lock

DK

Contents
Contenido

Welcome to the stable yard. This is where the horses eat and drink.

Bienvenidos al patio del establo. Aquí es donde los caballos comen y beben.

hay
heno

Pony
El poni

The pony has to be brushed and washed.

Al poni hay que cepillarlo y lavarlo.

brush
cepillo

grooming kit
kit de aseo
para caballos

Brown Horse
El caballo retinto

The brown horse has horseshoes fitted to its hooves.

Este caballo retinto tiene herraduras clavadas a sus cascos.

horseshoe
herradura

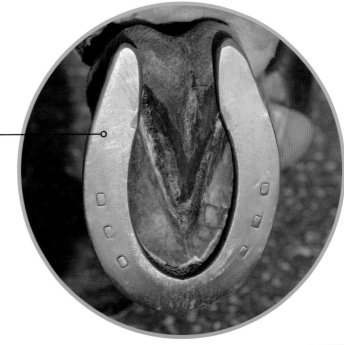

Palomino Pony
El poni palomino

The rider puts a saddle on the palomino pony.

La jinete pone una montura en el poni palomino.

saddle
montura

palomino pony
[pal-uh-MEE-no]

poni palomino

Chestnut Horses
Los caballos castaños

The chestnut horses go for a walk wearing bridles.
The riders wear riding hats.

A estos caballos castaños les ponen bridas para dar un paseo.
Los jinetes llevan cascos de montar.

bridle
brida

riding hat
casco de montar

15

Black Horse
El caballo negro

The black horse at the horse show performs tricks for people.

Este caballo negro le muestra sus habilidades a la gente en una exposición equina.

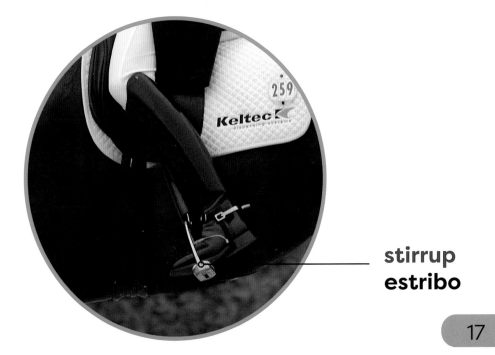

**stirrup
estribo**

Gray Pony
El poni gris

The rider tells
the gray pony to trot
and then to canter.

La jinete le pide al poni
gris que trote y, después,
que galope.

rider
jinete

Bay Horse
El caballo colorado

The reddish-brown bay horse jumps over the fence.

Este caballo colorado salta la valla.

fence
valla

Dancing Horses
Los caballos danzantes

The dancing horses jump and leap.

Los caballos danzantes saltan y brincan.

hooves
cascos

Racehorses
Los caballos de carreras

The racehorses race around the track. Who will win?

Los caballos de carreras corren por una pista. ¿Quién ganará?

jockey
jinete

track
pista

Ranch Horses
Los caballos de rancho

Ranchers ride ranch horses to round up the cattle.

Los rancheros usan caballos para reunir el ganado.

rancher
ranchero

cattle
ganado

Wild Horses
Los caballos salvajes

The wild horses gallop across a river.

Estos caballos salvajes galopan por un río.

Glossary
Glosario

brush
a tool for brushing the hair of a horse

fence
a row of bars for a horse to jump over

hooves
the feet of a horse

riding hat
a hard hat that a rider wears

saddle
a seat for a rider that is tied onto a horse's back

cascos
los pies de un caballo

casco de montar
gorro duro que se pone un jinete

cepillo
herramienta para cepillar el pelo de un caballo

montura
silla para un jinete que se amarra al lomo de un caballo

valla
fila de barras para que un caballo las salte

Index
Índice

Quiz
Prueba

Answer the questions to see what you have learned. Check your answers with an adult.

1. What is fitted to a horse's hooves?
2. What do a rider and horse do at a horse show?
3. What is the rider of a racehorse called?
4. What do ranchers and ranch horses do?
5. What would you like to do if you had your own horse? How would you take care of your horse?

1. Horseshoes 2. Perform tricks for people 3. A jockey 4. Round up cattle
5. Answers will vary

Responde las preguntas para saber cuánto aprendiste. Verifica tus respuestas con un adulto.

1. ¿Qué se clava a los cascos de un caballo?
2. ¿Qué hacen un jinete y su caballo en una exposición equina?
3. ¿Cómo se llama a quien monta caballos de carreras?
4. ¿Qué hacen los rancheros y los caballos de rancho?
5. ¿Qué te gustaría hacer si tuvieras un caballo? ¿Cómo cuidarías tu caballo?

1. Herraduras 2. Mostrarle a la gente sus habilidades 3. Jinete
4. Reunir el ganado 5. Las respuestas pueden variar.